FAMOUS LIVES

Inventors

Peggy Burns

WAYLAND

FAMOUS LIVES

Kings and Queens
Saints
Inventors
Explorers
Artists
Engineers

Cover pictures: (clockwise from top left) Thomas Edison, Alexander Graham Bell, James Watt.

Editor: Joanna Bentley
Designer: Joyce Chester
Consultant: Norah Granger

First published in 1996 by Wayland Publishers Limited,
61 Western Road, Hove, East Sussex, BN3 1JD

British Library Cataloguing in Publication Data
Burns, Peggy, 1941-
  Inventors.- (Famous Lives)
  1. Inventors - Biography - Juvenile literature
  2. Inventions - Juvenile literature
  I. Title
  609

ISBN 0 7502 1854 1

Typeset by Joyce Chester
Printed and bound by L.E.G.O. S.p.A., Vicenza, Italy

Picture Acknowledgements
The publishers wish to thank the following for allowing their photographs to be used in this book: AKG London 5, 18 (top), 19; Mary Evans Picture Library *cover* (Watt), 4, 6, 9 (top), 10, 11, 13, 15 (top), 18 (bottom); Hulton Deutsch Collection Ltd 14, 21 (both), 22, 24, 25, 26; Image Select 27; Ann Ronan at Image Select *cover* (background), 12, 16, 17; Visual Arts Library *cover* (Bell & Edison), title page, 8, 9 (bottom), 15 (bottom); Wayland Picture Library 7, 20; Zefa 23.

Contents

Johann Gutenberg

Six hundred years ago, books were not printed as they are today. Printing had not been invented in Europe at that time.

Books were rare and valuable. This was because each one had to be written by hand. It sometimes took years to make just one book.

Johann Gutenberg, who lived in Germany in the 1400s, discovered how to print books by making lots of separate metal letters. The letters could be arranged into a page of words called a forme. Ink was spread over the forme and a sheet of paper was pressed on to it. The writing then showed up on the paper.

◁ *Johann Gutenberg holding a block of letters for printing.*

Gutenberg wanted to build a printing press.
He did not have enough money to buy
equipment, so he borrowed money from
his partner, Johann Fust.

△ *This is the printing press Gutenberg built in 1455.*

In 1455 Gutenberg built his press. He decided to
print Bibles first. The Bibles had more than 1,000
pages. Printing them took a long time.
At last, the Bible was nearly ready.

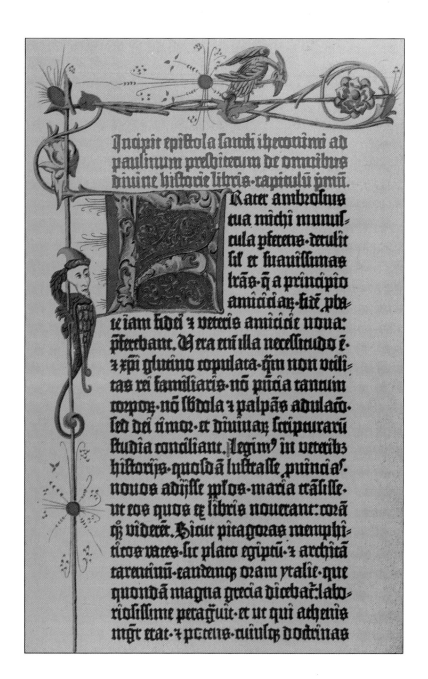

DATES

About **1400** Johann
Gutenberg born
1455 Gutenberg builds
his printing press
1468 Death of Gutenberg

◁ *A page from
Gutenberg's Bible.*

Suddenly, Fust decided he wanted his money
back. But Gutenberg could not pay him until the
Bibles were printed and sold!

Fust would not wait. He made Gutenberg give
him his printing press and all his equipment.
Then Fust went ahead and finished the Bibles
himself.

Johann Gutenberg did not make any money from his great invention. When he died in 1468 he was very poor.

But printed books and papers brought great changes to the world. It is thanks to Gutenberg that today we have the chance to learn to read and write.

△ *Today, thousands of newspapers can be printed in just one hour.*

James Watt

When he was a boy, James Watt enjoyed making and mending things. He had his own workbench in a corner of his father's workshop.

△ *James Watt as a boy, playing with steam from a kettle.*

When he grew up he went to work at Glasgow University. One day in 1763 he was asked to mend a model steam engine that was broken.

Watt looked closely at the engine he had been asked to mend. The steam engines in those days did not work very well. They did not make much power, and heating water to make the steam took huge amounts of coal.

An early steam engine used to stop mines from flooding. ▷

△ *James Watt working in his laboratory.*

Watt thought a lot about this problem. While he was taking a walk one Sunday afternoon, he suddenly thought of a different way to make steam engines work.

Watt planned to build a much better engine. It would use less coal and give more power.

Right away he started work on building his new engine. It was very rough because he built it so quickly. But it worked very well. That first steam engine built by James Watt still exists today.

◁ *This is Watt's steam engine, which worked better than the one on page 9.*

Watt worked on improving his engine. He invented a way of linking the steam engine to a wheel so that it could drive machinery.

Suddenly, all kinds of new inventions became possible. The steam train was developed and railway lines were built across the country. Steam engines could now drive machinery in factories and mills.

Those were years of great changes and wonderful inventions. We call that time the Industrial Revolution. James Watt's steam engine played a very important part in those changes.

△ *Steam power was used for lots of new inventions, including steam trains.*

DATES

1736 James Watt born
1765 Watt builds his steam engine
1819 Death of James Watt

Alexander Graham Bell

Alexander Graham Bell was born in Scotland in 1847. His mother was deaf, and his father taught deaf people to speak. So Alexander himself was very interested in how sounds are made and heard. When he was still a boy he made a model to show how the human voice worked.

◁ *Alexander Graham Bell in a lecture hall talks to his assistant in the basement using his telephone.*

DATES

1847 Alexander Graham Bell born
1876 The first words spoken over the telephone
1922 Death of Bell

When Alexander grew up he went to live in the USA. Bell believed it was possible to send the sound of someone speaking along a wire. He began to experiment with his ideas.

Bell built a model which sent electrical signals along a wire which led from one room to another. When he spoke into one end of the model, his assistant could hear his voice in the next room. 'Mr Watson, come here – I want you,' Bell said. Mr Watson heard him.

This man is using an early version of Bell's telephone equipment. ▽

Bell called his invention a telephone. His words to Mr Watson were the very first to be spoken over the telephone.

This was in March, 1876. Bell improved his invention, and by the end of the year telephone calls could be made over a distance of 229 kilometres (about 140 miles). Soon, they could go even further. It was not long before people in many American cities had telephones.

△ *In 1892 Bell opened the telephone link between the American cities New York and Chicago.*

Bell visited Europe to give talks on how the telephone worked. By 1891 telephone cables laid under the sea made it possible for people in Britain and other European countries to telephone each other.

This early telephone looks very different from the ones we use today. ▷

Alexander Graham Bell invented many other things, but the telephone is believed to be his greatest invention. He died in 1922. By 1932 there were almost 30 million telephones around the world.

◁ *Bell's invention of the telephone means that we can talk to people all around the world.*

Thomas Alva Edison

Thomas Alva Edison had always enjoyed making things. When he was ten years old he set up his own workshop in the basement of his family's house. Thomas did not go to school; his mother gave him lessons at home.

DATES

1847 Thomas Alva Edison born
1879 Edison's first successful demonstration of electric lights
1931 Death of Edison

◁ *Thomas Edison aged about 14.*

These oil lamps in the streets of London in the 1850s had to be refilled regularly. ▷

The world Thomas Edison grew up in was a much darker place than it is today. At that time, city streets and houses were lit by gas.

Some people still used candles or oil lamps to light their homes, especially in the country. The light from these was very dim.

Arc lights were the only kind of electric lighting. Arc lights were very expensive so people could not afford to light their houses with them. Thomas Edison thought he could find a way to make cheaper electric lights.

In his laboratory Edison used electricity to light up tiny wires, called filaments, inside a small glass bulb. His ideas worked: he had made an electric light bulb.

△ *Edison stands proudly in his laboratory with his light bulb.*

△ *Here Edison is working on his phonograph – an early kind of record player.*

◁ *Edison's light system was displayed as part of an early electricity exhibition.*

In 1879 Edison invited a few men to see his new invention. He switched on the light bulbs. They lit up, grew very bright – then went out. Edison was very disappointed. But he kept on working. At last, all went well.

On Christmas Eve, 1879, huge crowds of people came to his laboratory to see the wonderful new lights that lit the room brilliantly at the flick of a switch.

Electric lighting made Thomas Edison famous. But he went on thinking up new ideas. In his lifetime he made 1,000 inventions.

Wilbur and Orville Wright

For thousands of years people have wanted to fly like birds. Long ago, men sometimes made themselves wings from wood or feathers. They jumped off cliffs or towers and tried to fly. Most of them were killed.

Then the hot-air balloon was invented in 1783. At last, people could fly. But they could only go where the wind took them.

Two men who longed to fly were brothers, Wilbur and Orville Wright. They lived in the USA 100 years ago. They read every book they could find about flying.

◁ *The first crossing of the English Channel by air was in a hot-air balloon in 1785.*

In 1900 they built a glider. It was rather like a kite, but it was large enough to carry a man. They took their glider to Kitty Hawk, a small place by the sea. There were miles of sand, so it was ideal for their flying experiments.

The glider flew for a few seconds with Wilbur on board. The brothers were very pleased. Soon they could build a machine that could really fly.

△ *The Wright brothers' glider flying at Kitty Hawk in 1902.*

They went on with their experiments, improving their glider all the time. They tested new wings and added a different tail. By 1902 it was working well. All that was needed was an engine.

Finding the right kind of engine was not easy. In the end the Wrights made one themselves. At last, the flying machine was ready to try out.

On 17 December 1903 at Kitty Hawk, Orville Wright flew their aeroplane 40 metres. The brothers were very excited. They had made the very first engine-powered flight! They went on improving the plane. By 1905 they had built one that was bigger and more powerful. It flew 40 kilometres (nearly 25 miles).

△ *Orville Wright makes history in the first powered flight in 1903.*

△ *The Wright brothers did not live to see the huge, fast planes of today. They would have been thrilled to see Concorde, which flies faster than sound can travel!*

DATES

1867 Wilbur Wright born
1871 Orville Wright born
1903 The Wright brothers make the first powered flight
1912 Death of Wilbur Wright
1948 Death of Orville Wright

John Logie Baird

It was 1923, and people could buy a wonderful new invention called the radio. Although it was amazing to be able to hear sounds on this new radio, scientists believed that radio waves could be made to do even more than produce sound. Perhaps they could make pictures as well.

Inventors had been experimenting with the idea of television since about 1890, but could not find a way to make it work properly. One man, John Logie Baird, thought he knew how to do it.

△ *John Logie Baird.*

DATES

1888 John Logie Baird born

1926 Baird demonstrates television to a group of scientists

1946 Death of Baird

He could not afford expensive equipment, but he did not let that stop him.

Baird used a wooden tea-chest, a biscuit tin and a few cycle lamp lenses to make his first television camera.

They were all fixed together with bits of wood and string. But his ideas worked, and he was thrilled when at last his amazing invention sent a flickering picture across the room.

Baird working with equipment that would transmit the image of his face. ▽

Baird worked hard on improving his design, and a year later he was able to demonstrate television to a group of 50 scientists. By 1927 he could send television pictures across the Atlantic from London to New York using radio waves.

△ *John Logie Baird demonstrating his television transmitter on the roof of his laboratory.*

△ *One of the earliest television sets for home use.*

Britain set up the world's first television service in 1936. Television became popular after 1950, because by then sets were cheaper and more people could buy them.

Today, it is possible to watch television 24 hours every day, in brilliant colour. Most families around the world own at least one television set.

Timeline

Year	Inventor	How long ago?
1400	Johann Gutenberg born in Germany	600 years ago
1428	Gutenberg first experiments with printing	
1450		550 years ago
1455	Gutenberg sets up a printing press with Johann Fust	
1456	Gutenberg's press prints the first 300 Bibles	
1468	Death of Gutenberg	
1500		500 years ago
1550		450 years ago
1600		400 years ago
1650		350 years ago
1700		300 years ago
1736	James Watt born in Scotland	
1750		250 years ago
1754	Watt trains as an instrument maker	
1765	Watt invents his steam engine	
1800		200 years ago
1819	Death of James Watt	
1847	Alexander Graham Bell born in Scotland	
1847	Thomas Alva Edison born in USA	
1850		150 years ago

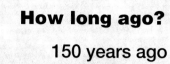
Year	Inventor	How long ago?
1850		150 years ago
1864	Edison makes his first invention	
1866	Bell becomes a teacher of deaf children	
1867	Wilbur Wright born in USA	
1871	Orville Wright born in USA	
1875	Bell invents the telephone	
1879	Edison demonstrates his electric lighting	
1888	John Logie Baird born in Scotland	
1896	Wright brothers begin experimenting with gliders	
1900		100 years ago
1903	Wright brothers make the first engine-powered flight	
1912	Death of Wilbur Wright	
1922	Death of Alexander Graham Bell	
1926	Baird invents television	
1931	Death of Thomas Edison	
1946	Death of Baird	
1948	Death of Orville Wright	
1950		50 years ago

29

Words to look up

Aeroplane An aircraft with wings and an engine.

Cable A wire that carries electricity.

Coal A hard, black rock that is burnt to make heat.

Code A set of signals used to send messages.

Craftsman A person who is very skilled in making things.

Demonstrate To show how something works.

Engineer A person who designs and makes machines of all kinds, or who builds roads and bridges.

Equipment Everything needed for a particular purpose.

Experimenting Testing ideas and studying the results.

Forme Metal letters arranged into a page for printing.

Glider A plane without an engine.

Industrial Revolution The time during the 18th and 19th centuries when Britain and other countries began to use machinery for producing goods.

Laboratory A room where scientific experiments are made.

Mills Buildings with machinery where goods, such as cloth, are made.

Transmit To send from one place to another.

Water wheel A wheel that is turned by water falling on to it, which produces power to run a machine.

Windmill A machine for grinding flour, etc, that is powered by the wind turning its sails.

Other books to look at

Facts at your Fingertips – Inventors by David Marshall, Simon & Schuster Young Books, 1992

Famous Inventors by Douglas McTavish, Wayland 1993

Science Discoveries – Thomas Edison and Electricity by Steve Parker, Belitha Press, 1992

Science Discoveries – Alexander Graham Bell and the Telephone by Steve Parker, Belitha Press, 1994

Inventions in Science – Flying Machines by Steve Parker, Aladdin Books Ltd, 1993

Incredible Inventions by Philip Wilkinson, Dorling Kindersley, 1995

Some places to see

British Telecom Museum, London has extensive displays about Alexander Graham Bell's invention of the telephone.

National Museum of Photography, Film and Television, Pictureville, Bradford, Yorkshire. Exhibits include John Logie Baird's original televison.

McLean Museum and Art Gallery, Greenock, Renfrewshire contains engine models and items connected with James Watt, who was born in Greenock.

The Gutenberg Museum, Mainz, Germany contains Gutenberg's original printing press.

The Science Museum, London - displays include copies of Bell's early telephones, a model of Gutenberg's press, several Edison lamps, Watt's garret workshop and some of his engines, and a copy of the Wright brothers' original Flyer.

Charlotte Square, Edinburgh. The house where Alexander Graham Bell was born is still there.

Index